IN HALF LIGHT
DALIA ELHASSAN

This is a work of fiction. All names, characters, places, and incidents are a product of the author's imagination. Any resemblance to real events or persons, living or dead, is entirely coincidental.

Published by Akashic Books

ISBN: 978-1-61775-742-6

Printed in China
First printing

Akashic Books
Brooklyn, New York, USA
Ballydehob, Co. Cork, Ireland
Twitter: @AkashicBooks
Facebook: AkashicBooks
E-mail: info@akashicbooks.com
Website: www.akashicbooks.com

African Poetry Book Fund
Prairie Schooner
University of Nebraska
110 Andrews Hall
Lincoln, Nebraska 68588

Table of Contents

Preface
by Safia Elhillo

With *In Half Light*, Dalia Elhassan holds us accountable for the ways we look
to a country to name us, and what is left behind when our countries fail to do
so—when they fail us. The first bit of verse we encounter in this collection is
the phrase, "tells me sudan has no place / for itself, says we are an extension / of
you," which, when read apart from its title and framing device—which identi-
fies an Egyptian girl as the one articulating this definition of the Sudan, trying
to wound—can function as a sort of statement of poetics for the collection
to come. Sudan is made and remade in these poems, mourned and critiqued
and protected "with our soul with our blood" (*art catalog of the sudanese*) and
populated, in the way stories of the Sudan told in English so rarely are, with
actual names—Rashid Diab, Benjamin Chokwan Ado, Kamala Ibrahim Ishaq,
and the speaker's jidu, among many others. And in this naming, a new sort of
country takes shape: a country where existing on a particular piece of land is no
longer a prerequisite for belonging, where the nation-state is obsolete as the site
for nationalism.

In *conversation about home*, Elhassan writes "i don't believe in nationalism
[…] feels like i'm every nation's castaway," and later revises this in *reclaiming the
tribe in seven accounts* with an image of the speaker's girl-self seated between her
mother's calves, having her hair braided and being reminded that "this is where
i come from." In this declaration, she confirms that having a country is no
longer a condition for having a home—that the people about whom she writes
with such gentleness, such compassion, can hold her and identify her in ways a
piece of land between borders never could. With these poems she invites us to
contend with our own understanding of nationalism, and is searing in the clar-
ity with which she writes about the ways in which loving a country implicates
us. *Conversations about home* declares, in the very first couplet, "i don't believe in
nationalism"—humbling the reader with the confidence in this declaration—
but then the poem closes with the speaker's confession that "even though the

flag has failed me / i am still raising it." The speaker implicates herself along with us, placing herself in community and conversation with us as we all parse these questions about belonging and nation and home, together—as we recognize how hard it is to shake off the countries through which we are used to identifying ourselves.

Elhassan's speaker is a historian in the tenderest sense, tracing Sudanese history and family history and Sudanese art history and a history of migration and exile and arrival, and all the ways these histories overlap and pull apart. She deftly unpeels layers of racism, of antiblackness, of the nuance often lacking in conversations around Blackness—"a girl in class asks / what part of me is black" (*reclaiming the tribe in seven accounts*). The sheer number of times the word "Sudanese" appears in this collection is its own music, and calls me, names me, with each and every occurrence. One of Elhassan's most stunning gifts is her commitment to naming, to populating a canon of her own, and locating herself in lineage. She names, among many others, the photographer Gadala Gubara, who made stunning portraits of Sudanese women, showcasing their shulookh scarring and the braids wound about their ears in the traditional way. With the directness and tenderness of his eye, he celebrated Sudanese womanhood and girlhood in their particularities and their expansiveness. Elhassan, as a poet, is similarly skilled and particular in her portraiture, in her centering and complication of Sudaneseness—in her empathy. The women she writes are resilient world-builders, countries without the failures of countries; and the men she writes are wounded, largely absent, but rendered with empathy and compassion and without judgement—held accountable but never condemned: "how many immigrant men come and lose / their lives/how many men sink" (*jidu (n.): origin, sudanese*).

In *art catalog of the sudanese*, she specifies her creative lineage, listing Sudanese artists throughout history, each line of the list beginning with the word "after," with the names in the last five lines of the list left blank—perhaps for those to come, those arriving after. The closing stanza of the poem breaks away from the list form and turns to address the Sudan directly, fiercely, lovingly:

with our soul with our blood
we will protect you, sudan
for our children
to see their history.

With this collection, with her poetics of naming and of documentation, Elhassan ensures that future generations of Sudanese—and with whatever "Sudan" itself will mean in the years ahead—will know those who came before, those who wrote and painted and made photographs so that our history can be traced clearly after so much erasure has been done to us.

black that holds up against language & sea
black the only name assigned my body
that ever felt like mine   black my hunted
kin   my hunted blood & black my only country...
>   —*asmar*, Safia Elhillo

Lineage/Where did they come from?
Bleeding down to her antecedents.
Written in block letter/Work with the
clutter of the un recollected . . .
No one travels between worlds like they used to.
>   —*Time Slips Right Before the Eyes*, Erica Hunt

the egyptian girl reads safia elhillo and all she can see is a reflection of her own people

tells me sudan has no place
for itself, says we are an extension
of you   we were never ours
      to keep

art catalog of the sudanese

after Rashid Diab

after Ibrahim El-Salahi

after Kamala Ibrahim Ishaq

after Fouad Hamza Tibin

after Gadala Gubara

after Abbas Habib Alla

after Ahmed Omar Addow

after Amin Rashid

after Djoua

after Madani A A Gahory

after Mohamed Abdarasul

after Mohamed Adam Anagha

after Mohamed Yahia Issa

after Omar Yahia Baram

after Osman Hamid

after Rashid Mahdi

after Richard Lokiden Wani

after Shogui

after Ahmed M. Shibrain

after Awad Eldaw

after Benjamin Chokwan Ado

after

after

after

after

after

with our soul with our blood

we will protect you, sudan

for our children

to see their history

conversation about home

after warsan

at a gathering i laugh and say
         i don't believe in nationalism.

the first time i go to sudan
         i arrive on a travel document,

green like the mountains
         i've never seen,

green like the second layer
         of the red sea.

i'm in a boat with my family
         five miles off the coast,

my cousins point to the ranges
         beneath the surface

& i think myself to be a mermaid,
         otherworldly, like the feeling i first felt

the first time my family meets me
         not in sudan,

not even at the border, but in cairo,
         on a boat just like this one,

my hands, skin older,
         still grazing the water.

i thought myself to be a mermaid then, too,
        but not like the little mermaid,

like her darker sister with the black hair,
        like the women on my mother's

side of the family. i wave
        a flag with their faces on it,

the closest thing to home,
        looks like an immigrant,

like the creases in my father's face,
        like the sunset touching miami,

like every mural of malcolm x
        in every diasporic city.

i never asked to leave, they took me.
        feels like i'm every nation's castaway.

mark of my mother's prayers.
        i sing songs to myself

in a dialect of arabic
        i'm constantly defending.

i liberate myself in a dialect
        i'm still defending.

even though the flag has failed me
        i am still raising it.

homecoming

i claim the corner seat
on the back of this pickup truck
with my uncles whose skins
are the color of freshly ground *bun*
and *habahan*

we're five hundred miles
east of the place where the white
and blue nile meet

i come from a country
where all we sing
are love songs
a country where all
the songs can be about love

or   my parents
            father not yet my baba
            seeing my mother
            and her fair skin
            for the first time

or   the first time she flashes
            him a smile/baba guiding
            a prayer through the gap
            between his two front teeth

or   my grandfather planting
            a pomegranate tree
            in the house my grandmother
            prays a family in

or   my uncle's beard
        pressing dimples onto
        my neck the first time
        he hugs me in twelve years

portrait titled after my father's absence

when I am 13, I ask my father to tell me the story of his life and he does not look
up from the bone to name a year: 1989. he was a young man in amreeka/امريكا for
the first time, first of his name to uproot the soil that raised him and 1989 is located
in nyc on an attic floor, meeting winter for the first time   and I take down the
details furiously: the ice that gathers on & flattens his afro, eyes that slowly lose
their warmth, button down short sleeve & corduroy pants, my father not yet my
father unhappy and alone in this country that does not forgive him or his father or
his father or his father for their existence   hope or pride his only faith,
years of watching sun become moon then sun again, snow that reveals what it
means to be white and the English he picks up is not the English of a colonial
school back home but a dialect easily mistaken as improper,   dialect that turns
and twists until tongue cannot tell native from foreign
            and I take this all in, note the details he does not mention—the failed
marriage to my mother and four kids he did not mind   loss of vision
and ability   feeling in his right knee   diabetes and the medication   loss of
nation-state   of omdurman   of what it means to truly be at home
of father   of self   lost, the only thing he feels   the only thing
he is to me

jidu (n.): origin, sudanese

the day my grandfather dies i am fast asleep
my mother wakes me up and her face is a wash of grief

i wonder what i can say for all the absent men in my life

i don't really remember him,
just the wrinkle beneath his left eyebrow,
the *'ilma* wrapped around his forehead

there are no shortages of sudanese men in america

men in their 1997 toyota camrys,
in the driver's seat of the cab,
behind the counter, cashier
half gentle-men

how many immigrant men come and lose
their lives/how many men sink

The Khartoum School: The Making of the Modern Art Movement in Sudan (1945–Present)

after Kamala Ibrahim Ishaq

a complex matrix of the social
primitive imagery
averted gazes of the viewer
the abstract dimension of faith
& spirituality

achieve sacredness
indicate sainthood
achieve
untitled composition

the Khartoum School:
a chronological journey
to elucidate the necessity
for cataloguing a history
disbanded in self-exile
& imprisonment
shape the course
of Sudan transparent
their vision of the universe
is subject position
in the world
is subject to change
accordingly

reclaiming the tribe in seven accounts

1.
i'm a year old the first time
my mother relaxes my hair

2.
at the masjid, a woman tells another
she isn't welcome here
because islam is a religion
for arabs

3.
a girl in class asks
what part of me is black

4.
i let the wind whip off
my hijab late last summer
on the sputtering back of a rickshaw

5.
sometimes i imagine
a sudan that isn't broken
not without a south
doesn't look shattered by two niles

6.
i come from two tribes
and two countries
a single foot in both worlds

7.
my body is the sum of all these histories
and i don't belong to anything
except
hip hop and

to my grandmother's kitchen
to every kitchen that became hers
to the cities that raised me
to the sky with the 3-5pm stretch
of sun drawn afternoon and palm trees
to the spot between my mother's
calves, my unbraided hair hanging
loose against them
her hands, weaving in and out of scalp
tugging my head back,
reminding me

this is where i come from

our deepest fear

i have forgotten what it is to be brilliant and the first time i learn the word from
marianne williamson i am on a coach bus coming home from an overnight pil-
grimage to universal studios i am in the fifth grade the only student awake riding
through the night in a seat too big my braids unkempt and *mankusha* like my
mother named me seeing akeelah on screen for the first time with her gaze fixed
beyond me past my cheek and the cool walls of this vehicle and my little body
curling in the seat seeing her with her tight braids and wire rimmed glasses like
mine extending her voice her hands her vision uprooting my childhood insecurities
teaching me

   how to spell my own name how to properly pronounce the hard
questions even though my english is good enough telling me to say

        who am i to be brilliant? say *who am I*
to make manifest? say *who am i to give and receive permission?* say *who am I*
when I am no longer afraid?

Open in the Spring

This morning I watched my mother
unfurl like a cherry blossom.

Her arms branched towards the ceiling,
weaving into the air, coiling.

Her back, arched like a bough,
dripped satin bed sheets.

Words piled beneath her bottom lip,
pulled back in a yawn.

Her teeth—white buds—wedged
themselves between sunlight and

her voice, raw honey—
drops of Arabic thickening in the heat.

In the afternoon, she sat like a mangrove,
her arms, roots submerged in cooking.

Her knees, reeds bent in the Egyptian
wind, rode the hardwood floors like leaves.

I wish I thanked her for reaching
into soil and watering down the world

before my eyes so like a banyan
I'd be able to grow from it.

This evening, I sit beneath my mother's feet.
She is a date tree, arms spread wide and thin as the
Nile.

الجنة تحت أقدام الأمهات
Heaven shadows itself in her footprints.

final portrait of the sudanese

my parents sit side-by-side
        in the half-light,

two bodies, a half-world
        away from me, singing

the way only sudanis know
        how to.

شوفي الزمن يا يمة
        ساقني بعيد خلاص .

shuf al-zaman ya yuma
        sayignee ba'eed khalas

look at this time, oh mama,
        its taken me so far

on the uptown 6 train.
        my father—in sudan

—calls to ask us how we're doing.
        are you okay? how's your mother?

my mother, in the Bronx,
        waiting for her children

to come home,
        to learn her mother's language.

i swallowed two other languages
        before downing my own,

gutted my throat
        of any accent

spent years tearing
        up maps of Africa

trying to rub the sandalwood
        musk from behind my ears.

i don't bother to learn
        the songs my parents sing,

instead i write poems,
        about our hyphenated bodies,

about the frankincense smoke
        dancing on hot coal

about their hands
        that never touch,

and all the ways
        i hardly recognize them.

Notes

"art catalog of the sudanese"
The lines "with our soul with our blood / we will protect you, sudan" are
from a clip in a documentary project titled *The Two Sudans* in which
protestors in Sudan chant "with our soul, with our blood, we will protect
you, oh Sudan." The lines "for our children / to see their history" are a direct
quote taken from Benjamin Chokwan Ado, one of the men named among
others in the dedication of the poem, from the Al Jazeera Witness film
Sudan's Forgotten Films.

"portrait titled after my father's absence"
The word "امريكا," phonetically spelled "amreeka," translates in English to
"America."

"The Khartoum School: The Making of the Modern Art Movement in
Sudan (1945–Present)"
The title of this poem refers to an art exhibit of the same name previously
on display at the Sharjah Art Foundation.

"our deepest fear"
The title of this poem refers to a quote by Marianne Williamson that goes
"Our deepest fear is not that we are inadequate. Our deepest fear is that we
are powerful beyond measure. It is our light, not our darkness, that most
frightens us."

"Open in the Spring"
The lines "الجنة تحت اقدام الامهات / Heaven shadows itself in her footprints"
refers to an Islamic hadith (saying) of Prophet Muhammed (pbuh) that
says "Heaven lies below the feet of your mother."

"final portrait of the sudanese"

The lines "ساقني بعيد خلاص شوفي الزمن يا يمة/ shuf al-zaman ya yuma /say-ignee ba'eed khalas" refer to a lyric from "بحر المودة (Bahr al Mawadda - Sea of Affection)" that translates to "look at the time, oh mama, its taken me so far."

Acknowledgments

A version of "Open in the Spring" first appeared in print and digitally in *The Kenyon Review.*

"final portrait of the sudanese" first appeared in *Rattle #59.*